FRIDAY

11/12/99

Wishing you a
very happy birthday,
Helyn! I treasure
your friendship.
May God's richest
blessings always be
yours!

Love,
Teona
Shana
Scott

This is the day the Lord has made; let us
rejoice and be glad in it.

Psalm 118:24

All Scripture is taken from the
New International Version of the Bible.

This is the day the Lord has made; let us
rejoice and be glad in it.
Psalm 118:24

And we know that in all things God works
for the good of those who love Him, who have been
called according to His purpose.
Romans 8:28

There is a time for everything, and a season for
every activity under heaven...
Ecclesiastes 3:1

But if we walk in the light, as He is in the light,
we have fellowship with one another...
1 John 1:7

Serve the Lord with gladness; come before
Him with joyful songs.
Psalm 100:2

Now faith is being sure of what we hope for and
certain of what we do not see.
Hebrews 11:1

God is our refuge and strength, an ever present
help in trouble.
Psalm 46:1

I can do everything through Him who
gives me strength.
Philippians 4:13

Pleasant words are a honeycomb, sweet to the soul
and healing to the bones...
Proverbs 16:24

...but if we love each other, God lives in us and His
love is made complete in us.
1 John 4:12

Delight yourself in the Lord and He will give you
the desires of your heart.
Psalm 37:4

"Everything is possible for him who believes."
Mark 9:23

Trust in the Lord with all your heart and lean not
on your own understanding...
Proverbs 3:5

"My soul praises the Lord and my spirit
rejoices in God my Savior..."
Luke 1:46,47

...but those who hope in the Lord will renew their
strength. They will soar on wings like eagles...

Isaiah 40:31

Be kind and compassionate to one another, forgiving
each other, just as in Christ God forgave you.
Ephesians 4:32

A friend loves at all times...
Proverbs 17:17

Whatever you do, work at it with all your heart,
as working for the Lord...
Colossians 3:23

Surely goodness and love will follow me all the
days of my life, and I will dwell in the house of
the Lord forever.
Psalm 23:6

> "Ask and it will be given to you; seek and you will
> find; knock and the door will be opened to you."
> Matthew 7:7

...stop and consider God's wonders.
Job 37:14

"...let your light shine before men, that they may
see your good deeds and praise your Father in heaven."
Matthew 5:16

> My heart took delight in all my work, and this was
> the reward for all my labor.
> Ecclesiastes 2:10

...let us love one another, for love comes from God.
1 John 4:7

The days of the blameless are known to the Lord,
and their inheritance will endure forever.
Psalm 37:18

But the fruit of the Spirit is love, joy, peace,
patience, kindness, goodness, faithfulness,
gentleness and self-control.

Galatians 5:22,23

Commit to the Lord whatever you do,
and your plans will succeed.
Proverbs 16:3

"Therefore do not worry about tomorrow,
for tomorrow will worry about itself."
Matthew 6:34

Teach us to number our days aright, that we may
gain a heart of wisdom.
Psalm 90:12

"...all things are possible with God."
Mark 10:27

He has made everything beautiful in its time.

Ecclesiastes 3:11

Be joyful in hope, patient in affliction,
faithful in prayer.
Romans 12:12

The Lord is my strength and my shield; my heart
trusts in Him, and I am helped.
Psalm 28:7

...whatever is lovely, whatever is admirable—
if anything is excellent or praiseworthy—
think about such things.
Philippians 4:8

A cheerful heart is good medicine...
Proverbs 17:22

Love does not delight in evil but rejoices with the
truth. It always protects, always trusts, always hopes,
always perseveres. Love never fails.

1 Corinthians 13:6-8

The Lord is my shepherd, I shall lack nothing. He makes
me lie down in green pastures, He leads me beside quiet
waters, He restores my soul.

Psalm 23:1-3

"Blessed are the pure in heart, for they will see God."
Matthew 5:8

"The Lord bless you and keep you; the Lord make His
face shine upon you and be gracious to you; the Lord
turn His face toward you and give you peace."
Numbers 6:24-26

In His great mercy He has given us new birth into a
living hope through the resurrection of Jesus Christ...
1 Peter 1:3

Friday 12 November 1999
Antonio's 7pm
Teona, Scott, Shana Johnson
Charley, Russ Ward
Cake
Richard Kopacz

TAVI - 5yrs old

Happy Birthday Ho-Ho, I hope you
have a nice day. Shana

Happy Birthday, so glad
to share this day with
you. our Friendship is
very special to me. Richi,

Happy Birthday Helyn & Tavi. Hope
you have a wonderful year.
                    Charley Ward
                    Cay Erde

MAY YOU HAVE MANY MORE WONDERFUL
ANNUAL CELEBRATIONS OF YOUR BIRTH!
I HOPE YOU ENJOYED TODAY. Russ